Sift and Shout

Sand Play Activities
For 1-6 Year Olds

Randy F. Granovetter
Jeanne C. James

Illustrations by: Tim Bailey
Craig Rogers

Other Books By The Authors:
A Planning Guide To The Preschool Curriculum
Waterworks
Learning In Pairs
*Our World: A Planning Guide For The Kindergarten
and First Grade Curriculum*

© 1989 Randy F. Granovetter and Jeanne C. James

Published by: Kaplan Press, Inc.
1310 Lewisville-Clemmons Road
Lewisville, NC 27023   ISBN # 0-88076-122-9

Dedication

For all of the children with sand in their shoes, especially Jo Anna, Brett and Jason. Your joy and growth in sand play inspired us.

To the dedicated adults who willingly clean up, so that children may engage in sand play.

Table of Contents

Introduction

We wrote this book because sand play provides fun and important learning opportunities for young children. Sand play activities can reinforce scientific ideas and mathematical concepts. Sand play is used to integrate cognitive, fine motor, and gross motor skills. Most children enjoy sand play activities and will engage in them readily. The activities in this book can be used by all teachers, caregivers, and parents to build skills with children in an enjoyable way.

Instructor's Guide

Before discussing the format of the book, we ask that you be certain to read the Safety Tips which follow the Instructor's Guide.

This book is organized into three sections. Each section consists of activities for a particular age group. These are:

> Activities for ones and twos;
> Activities for threes and fours;
> Activities for fives and sixes; and in addition to the three sections above there are craft activities for threes, fours, fives and sixes.

Within each age group section the activities are divided into four types. Each type of activity is represented by an icon in the upper outer corner. This is to make it easy to find the activity. If you have used Waterworks, you know how much easier it is to locate activities with the icons. The icon for these activities is:

Activities to be done with a small amount of sand by one or more children. They include pouring, patting and molding, drawing, and sand science. The icon for these activities is:

Activities for a sand table which can be done by one or more children. They include pouring, patting and molding, drawing, building castles, and games. The icon for this section is:

Activities for a sandbox which include drawing, building and sculpting, and games. The icon for these activities is:

Activities for the beach which include building and sculpting and movement activities. Some of these activities may be adaptable to a sand box. The icon for these activities is:

The final section of activities is unique in that it spans age groups three through six. It is a group of craft ideas that involve sand. Sand lends itself well to crafts, and we felt it necessary to include some craft ideas in this book. The craft activity pages have the following icon, so you can find them quickly.

Familiarity with the logos will help you to locate particular activities quickly.

Note that some of the pan, sandbox and sand table activities could be interchanged.

Safety Tips

Always have an adult with the child or children in any sand play situation, especially at the beach. NEVER LEAVE A CHILD UNATTENDED.

Use only unbreakable materials for sand play activities. NEVER USE GLASS, CERAMIC, PORCELAIN, POTTERY, CHINA OR OTHER BREAKABLE MATERIALS.

Always gather materials ahead of time, so you do not have to leave the child or children unattended.

Develop sand play rules with the children. Discuss and generate a list that is appropriate to your situation and revise them as needed. For example, you will need one set of rules when the children are playing at the sand table and other rules for the beach.

    Some ideas for rules include:
        Keep all sand below eye level.
        No throwing sand.
        Keep the sand in the containers.
        When pouring sand, keep it below eye level.
        Sweep up spills immediately.

Supervise children carefully and remind them of the sand play rules.

Explain and discuss sand play rules with the children.

Materials

Many of the materials used in sand play are found objects such as empty containers, cups, measuring caps from coffee and drink mixes, styrofoam trays, styrofoam pieces, rocks, shells, etc. In a day care or nursery setting parents can save these materials for use by the children. Clean materials which had food or chemicals thoroughly.

Other materials are readily available from local sources. These include construction paper, scissors, tape, tongue depressors, plastic measuring cups, styrofoam cups, dishpans, screens, sieves, shovels, buckets, beach balls, etc. Check local discount, grocery, and hardware stores.

Other materials will have to be purchased from specialized sources such as school supply catalogs. This includes materials such as dry tempera paint, sand tables, sand sifters, etc.

Always gather all the materials for an activity before you begin so that you will not have to leave the children alone to get them.

ACTIVITIES FOR
ONE AND TWO YEAR OLDS

Pouring
Back, Forth, Through

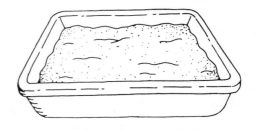

Materials:

- Pan - half full of sand
- Scoops
- Clear, plastic cups with and without handles
- Funnels
- Sand sieves

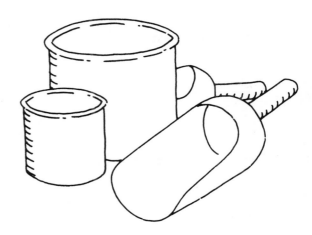

Materials Preparation:

None

Activity:

The child:

- Scoops up sand and pours it into a plastic cup.
- Continues scooping sand into the cup until the cup is full.
- Fills other plastic cups.
- Empties plastic cups from one to another or into pan.
- Pours sand into a funnel placed on a clear plastic cup.
- Observes the sand go through the funnel.
- Pours sand into a sand sieve placed on a clear, plastic cup.
- Observes the sand go through the sand sieve.

The adult:

- Places plastic cups in the sand pan.
- Encourages the child to fill the plastic cups.
- Helps child notice when the cup is full, *"The cup is **full**."*
- When the child empties the cup, notes *"The cup is **empty**."*
- Places a funnel on a clear, plastic cup.
- Notices that the sand goes **through** the funnel.

Things To Think About

Basic Skills: Pouring from one container to another. Learning about full and empty. Learning about through.

Patting and Molding
Fill 'er Up

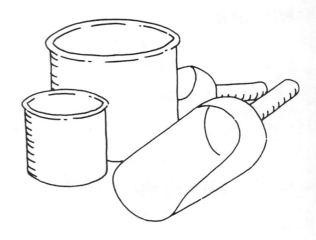

Materials:

• Cups or molds (different sizes)
• Deep pan
• Sand
• Scoops (different sizes)
• Water

Materials Preparation:

• Mix some water into the sand to make it good molding consistency.

Activity:

The child:

• Fills scoop with sand.
• Pours sand into cup or mold.
• Pats sand into cup or mold with hand.
• Turns cup over to show sand mold.

The adult:

• Reviews sand rules.
• Demonstrates the steps of how to make a mold.

Things To Think About

Basic Skills: Pouring, grasping, and patting.

12

Drawing Parallel Tracks

Materials:

- Popsicle sticks or tongue depressors
- Deep pan
- Sand

Materials Preparation:

None

Activity:

The child:

- Holds stick in hand.
- Watches adult make straight or curved stroke.
- Makes similar stroke under adult's stroke.

The adult:

- Draws a straight line or a curved line with a stick.

Things To Think About

Basic Skills: Grasping and drawing. Learning the ideas of curved and straight.

Sand Science
Coloring Sand

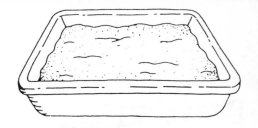

Materials:

- Sand
- Red, green, blue and black tempera powder
- Clear cups
- Scoops
- Spoons
- Paper

Materials Preparation:

None

Activity:

The child:

- Scoops a small amount of sand into a cup.
- Picks one color tempera powder.
- Puts a spoon of the tempera powder into the cup of sand.
- Stirs the tempera powder into the sand.
- Observes how the sand looks colored.
- Spreads a small amount of the sand out on paper and looks at it.

The adult:

- Demonstrates stirring the tempera powder and sand.
- Points out that the sand looks the color of the tempera powder.

Things To Think About

Basic Skills: Making choices, stirring, and observing.

14

Pouring
Did I Fill One or Two?

Materials:

- Sand table
- Plastic containers for filling with sand

Materials Preparation:

None

Activity:

The child:

- Hands adult one or two containers as requested.
- Fills the container(s) with sand.
- Watches as adult counts containers.
- Pours the sand out.
- Repeats process with more containers.

The adult:

- Requests the child to select one or two containers.
- Counts the containers after the child fills them.
- Encourages and helps the child continue.

Things To Think About

The younger child may not be able to select one or two, so guide him to pick the correct number.

Basic Skill: Identifying one or two objects.

Patting and Molding
Making Mountains

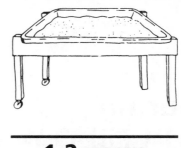

Materials:

• Sand table
• Water

Materials Preparation:

• Mix some water into the sand to make it good packing consistency.

Activity:

The child:

• Pushes and pulls sand together with his hands to create mountain shapes.
• Uses fingers to sculpture mountain surfaces.
• Creates a variety of mountains - some big and some little.
• Responds to question "How big is the mountain?" by showing size with hands.

The adult:

• Helps the child create mountain shapes.
• Helps the child sculpture mountain surfaces.
• Helps the child identify big mountains and little mountains.
• Asks "How big?"
• Models showing mountain size with hands and saying "So big."

Things To Think About

The one-two year old child may not necessarily identify big and little, but the adult should point out those ideas. The two year old child can make horizontal, vertical, and V-shaped designs.

Basic Skills: Patting and molding. Sculpting with fingers and hands. Identifying big and little.

Drawing
Connect The Dots

1-2 years

Materials:

- Popsicle sticks
- Sand table
- Sand

Materials Preparation:

None

Activity:

The child:

- Draws a straight line with a popsicle stick or finger between the dots to connect them.
- Draws a curved line to connect the dots.

The adult:

- Makes dots on a straight path in the sand.
- Makes dots on a curved path in the sand.
- Makes dots on a circular path in the sand.
- Guides child's hand to connect the dots.

Things To Think About

Basic Skills: Grasping and drawing. The concepts of curved and straight.

Building Tower of Two

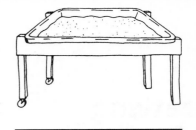

Materials:

- Sand table
- Small cups or molds
- Water

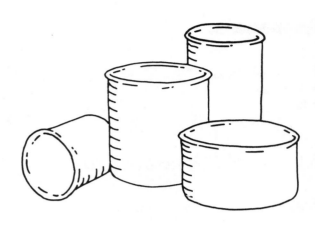

Materials Preparation:

- Mix some water into the sand to make it good molding consistency.

Activity:

The child:

- Fills two small cups or molds with sand.
- Packs the sand tightly into the molds.
- Turns the mold over in the sand table for the first mold in the tower.
- Turns a second mold over on top of the first.

The adult:

- Helps the child fill molds.
- Helps the child pack the sand tightly.
- Helps the child turn the mold over in the sand table.
- Helps the child turn the second mold over on top of the first.
- Counts the molds as they work, but does not expect the child to count.

Things To Think About

The child is not ready to count at this stage, so do not expect him to do so. Some children may build higher towers.

Basic Skills: Filling and patting. Lining things up when stacking. Creating a tower with two things.

Castles
Cup Castles

Materials:

- Cups (different sizes)
- Sand table
- Sand
- Scoops (different sizes)

Materials Preparation:

None

Activity:

The child:

- Scoops sand into two cups of different sizes.
- Pats sand tightly in cup.
- Turns larger cup of sand over first.
- Turns smaller cup of sand over next on top of the larger sand mold.
- Continues to build one and two cup high structures to create a castle.

The adult:

- Demonstrates how to make a cup mold.
- Encourages child to create a castle.

Things To Think About

Basic Skills: Grasping, patting, and molding.

Games
Treasure Treasure

Materials:

- Sand table
- Small objects (safe for 1-2 year olds)

Materials Preparation:

None

Activity:

The child:

- Digs hole in the sand.
- Watches adult place object in hole.
- Finds object in hole.
- Watches adult partially bury object.
- Finds object and removes it gently from the sand.

The adult:

- Encourages and helps child dig hole in the sand.
- Places object in hole while child watches.
- As child catches on to the idea that the object will be there, buries part of the object under sand.
- Encourages and helps child find object.

Things To Think About

Basic Skill: Reinforcement of idea that the object exists even if it cannot be seen (Piaget's Object Permanence).

Drawing
Who Do I Match?

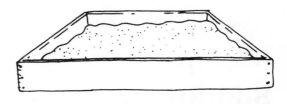

Materials:

- Sandbox full of sand
- Tools for drawing in sand such as rakes and hoes
- Pairs of objects for the children to connect

Materials Preparation:

- Prepare or locate pairs of objects for the children to connect.

Activity:

The child:

- Selects a pair of matching objects.
- Lays them in the sandbox some distance apart.
- Uses a rake, hoe, or other tool to make a path connecting the two objects.
- Moves one object to the other along the path.

The adult:

- Smooths the sand in the sandbox.
- Divides it into areas for children to use.
- Helps children select objects to connect.
- Helps children connect objects.

Things To Think About

Basic Skills: Matching two objects. Making a line with a tool. Following a path.

Building and Sculpting
Drive a Train

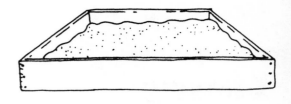

Materials:

• Sandbox
• Small wooden or plastic train

Materials Preparation:

None

Activity:

The child:

• Smooths the sand in the sandbox.
• Builds a flat, straight and curved roadbed in the sand.
• Pushes the train on the predrawn tracks in the sand.

The adult:

• Pushes the train several times on the flat roadbed to make tracks.

Things To Think About

Basic Skills: Development of eye-hand coordination. Building concepts of straight and curved.

22

Games
Guess Whose Foot?

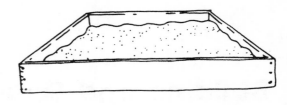

Materials:

• Sandbox

Materials Preparation:

None

Activities:

The children:

• Take off their shoes and socks.
• Each child makes a footprint in the sand.
• Walk around the footprints and place their feet in other children's and adult's footprints until they find their own.
• Each child compares the size (bigger, smaller, or same) of her feet to the others.
  and
• Compare shoes to decide which are bigger and smaller.

The adult:

• Makes his footprint in the sand.
• Shows children different footprints and compares his foot size emphasizing whether the foot or the footprint is bigger, smaller, or the same.
• Makes certain differences in size are very obvious.

Things To Think About

One and two year olds will have trouble making distinctions so the adult needs to point out the bigger and smaller. Also the adult should make certain that the size differences are significant.

Basic Skills: Removing shoes and socks. Learning the words bigger, smaller, and same.

Building and Sculpting A Village

Materials:

- Beach
- Bucket
- Many different shaped containers
- Tubes (toilet paper and paper towel)
- Shovels or large spoons
- Shells

Materials Preparation:

None

Activity:

The child:

- Packs containers with moist sand.
- Turns them over on the beach.
- Repeats until there are a variety of "dwellings."
- Uses shells to decorate the structures.
- Uses tubes to join the structures.

The adult:

- Encourages the children to pack the sand tightly.
- Encourages the children to work in close proximity so that their buildings will form a village.
- Talks about "dwellings" seen in a village.

Things To Think About

Basic Skills: Packing and molding sand. Working in close proximity with other children.

24

Movement
Footprints In The Sand

1-2 years

Materials:

• Beach

Materials Preparation:

None

Activity:

The child:

• Makes footprints in the sand by standing.
• Looks at the footprints.
• Makes footprints in the sand by walking forward.
• Looks at the footprints.
• Compares them to the footprints made when standing.
• Makes footprints in the sand by walking backward.
• Looks at the footprints.
• Compares them to the footprints made when standing and walking forward.
• Makes footprints in the sand by jumping.
• Looks at the footprints.
• Compares them to the footprints made when standing and walking forward and backward.

The adult:

• Models walking forward and backward and jumping.
• Helps child compare different footprints.

Things To Think About

Basic Skill: Developing balance skills.

ACTIVITIES FOR
THREE AND FOUR YEAR OLDS

Pouring
Pour and Sift

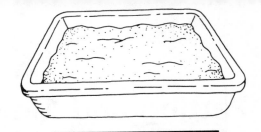

Materials:

- Pan - half full of sand
- Scoops
- Clear, plastic cups with and without handles
- Funnels
- Sand sieves

Materials Preparation:

None

Activity:

The child:

- Scoops up sand and pours it into a plastic cup.
- Pours sand into a funnel placed on a clear plastic cup.
- Observes the sand go through the funnel.
- Pours sand into a sand sieve placed on a clear, plastic cup.
- Observes the sand go through the sand sieve.
- Selects two cups that are the **same.**
- Uses the funnel to fill them to the same level.
- Observes that they are the same.
- Repeats with **different** levels of sand and **different** cups.

The adult:

- Notices that the sand goes **through** the funnel.
- Notices which cups are the **same**.
- Notices which cups are **different**.

Things To Think About

Basic Skills: Pouring from one container to another. Learning about through. Learning about same and different.

Patting and Molding Mini to Maxi Molds

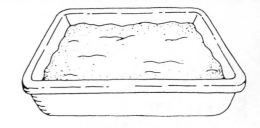

Materials:

- Cups or molds (different sizes)
- Deep pan
- Sand
- Scoops
- Water

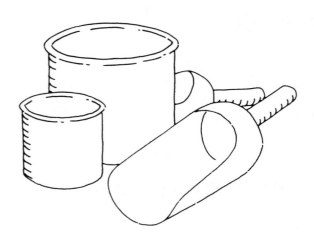

Materials Preparation:

- Mix some water into the sand to make it good molding consistency.

Activity:

The child:

- Fills scoop with sand.
- Pours sand into cup or mold.
- Pats sand into cup or mold with hand.
- Turns cups or molds over in sequential order to show sand molds of different sizes or to make a sequential tower.

The adult:

- Lines molds up in sequential order by size with the child.

Things To Think About

Basic Skills: Pouring, patting, grasping, and patting. Learning concepts of size and sequential order.

Drawing Monster Faces

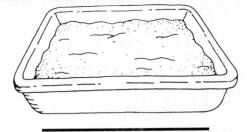

Materials:

• Popsicle sticks
• Deep pan
• Sand

Materials Preparation:

None

Activity:

The child:

• Draws a monster's face in the sand with a stick.
• Uses sticks half buried in the sand for monster tentacles, hair, or other monster facial features.

The adult:

• Demonstrates how to use popsicle sticks as a facial feature.

Things To Think About

Basic Skills: Identifying facial features.

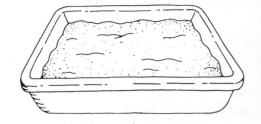

Sand Science
Is The Sand Different Sizes?

Materials:

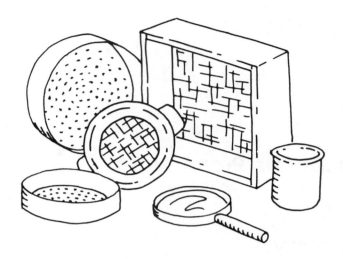

- Beach sand, if possible
- Screens, sieves, or sifters with different-sized holes
- White paper
- Magnifying glass

Materials Preparation:

None

Activity:

The child:

- Sorts the screens, sieves, or sifters by hole size.
- Puts some sand in the smallest sieve.
- Shakes gently onto a piece of white paper.
- Transfers the sand which remains into the next larger sieve over a new piece of paper.
- Shakes gently.
- Repeats with all sieves with progressively larger sized holes.
- Looks at sand on each piece of paper with a magnifying glass.

The adult:

- Helps the children order screens, sieves, and sifters by hole size.
- Shows children how to look through a magnifying glass.

Things To Think About

Basic Skills: Ordering by size, sifting gently, and looking through a magnifying glass.

32

Pouring
What Does Sand Go Through?

Materials:

- Sand table
- Plastic containers for filling with sand
- Sieves, funnels, vegetable spoons and other things that sand may or may not go through
- Screen, net, and other materials that sand may or may not go through
- Guide chart for sorting

Materials Preparation:

- Make a guide chart for children to sort sand permeable from nonpermeable items.

Activity:

The child:

- Fills container with sand.
- Places funnel, sieve, or other material over the sand table.
- Attempts to pour sand through a variety of items and materials.
- Sorts items and materials into two stacks - those that sand goes through and those it doesn't.

The adult:

- Encourages and helps child experiment.
- Helps child sort items and materials into two stacks - those that sand goes through and those it doesn't.

Things To Think About

Basic Skill: Developing idea that sand goes through some things and not through others.

Patting and Molding Sand Caterpillar

Materials:

- Sand table
- Water
- Popsicle sticks
- Feathers

Materials Preparation:

- Mix some water into the sand to make it good packing consistency.

Activity:

The child:

- Pulls sand together with his hands to create a caterpillar.
- Uses fingers and hands to sculpture two or more body sections of caterpillar.
- Uses his hands to create a round head.
- Uses fingers or popsicle sticks to make circle eyes and V-shaped mouth.
- Places feathers to represent feelers.
- Makes many caterpillars — some long and some short.
- Identifies the big and little caterpillars.
- Compares caterpillars — which are big and which are little.

The adult:

- Helps the child create caterpillar shapes.
- Helps the child sculpture body sections of caterpillar and head.
- Helps the child use tools to make eyes and mouth.
- Helps the child identify the big and little caterpillars.
- Helps the child compare caterpillars — big and little.

Things To Think About

The 3-4 year old child is interested in big and little.

Basic Skills: Patting and molding. Sculpting with fingers, hands, and tools. Identifying long and short. Making circles and V-shapes.

Drawing Patterns In The Sand

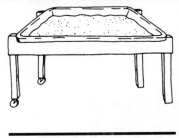

Materials:

- Markers
- Paper
- Candy apple sticks
- Sand table
- Sand

Materials Preparation:

None

Activity:

The child:

- Creates a design on paper with markers.
- Smoothes sand.
- Places the paper design on top of the sand.
- Using a candy apple stick, pokes holes in the paper along the border of the design.
- Removes the paper and draws the design in the sand with finger or stick.

The adult:

- Shows the child how to poke holes in the paper design when it is on top of the sand.

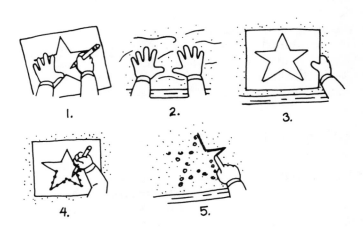

Things To Think About

Use this activity to reinforce any shape concepts you are teaching.

Basic Skills: Grasping, drawing and following a pattern.

Building Tall Towers

Materials:

- Sand table
- Small cups or molds
- Tongue depressors or popsicle sticks
- Water

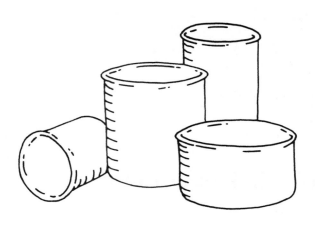

Materials Preparation:

- Mix some water into the sand to make it good molding consistency.

Activity:

The child:

- Fills molds with sand.
- Packs the sand tightly into the molds.
- Turns the molds over in the sand table one on top of the other to create a tower.
- Counts the number of molds in the tower with the adult's help.
- Makes several towers.
- Decides which tower is taller.
- Decides which tower is shorter.
- Counts the number of towers.

The adult:

- Helps the child fill molds.
- Helps the child pack the sand tightly.
- Helps the child turn the molds over in the sand table to create towers.
- Helps the child count the molds as he works.
- Helps the child decide which tower is taller.
- Helps the child decide which tower is shorter.
- Helps the child count towers.

Things To Think About

The child may not be able to count accurately at this stage, so do not expect him to do so. The activity is designed to build fine motor and eye-hand coordination skills. Because the activity is so concrete, it can be used to teach comparatives and some counting, but counting is not the emphasis.

Basic Skills: Developing the fine motor skills of filling and patting. Developing the eye-hand coordination skills of lining things up when stacking. Creating a tower. Identifying taller and shorter. Developing some beginning counting skills.

Castles
Drip Castles

Materials:

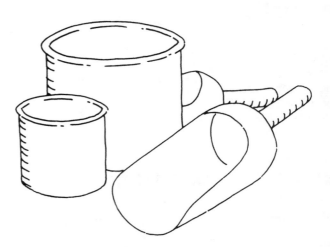

- Bucket
- Cups (different sizes)
- Sand table
- Sand
- Scoops (different sizes)
- Water

Materials Preparation:

None

Activity:

The child:

- Scoops one scoop of sand into a bucket of water.
- Takes a hand full of sand and water.
- Lets the sand drip off of his hand into the sand table.
- Repeats this procedure until he has built a drip castle in the sand table.

The adult:

- Demonstrates how to drip with wet sand.

Things To Think About

Basic Skills: Grasping, scooping, and cupping hands.

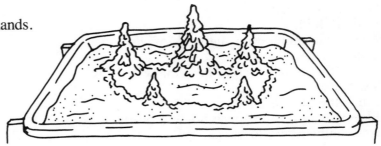

Games
How Many Did I Hide?

Materials:

- Sand table
- Small objects (safe for 3-4 year olds) such as teddy bear counters
- Counting cards with numerals from one to five (See materials preparation.)

Materials Preparation:

- Make counting cards with numerals from one to five on one side and that number of space holders on the other side. (See Illustration.)
- Laminate the cards to increase their life.

Activity:

The children:

- One child hides his eyes.
- The other child:
  Selects a counting card.
  Places an appropriate number of objects on the space holders.
  Then buries the objects in the sand.
  Shows the first child the numeral on the counting card.
  Verifies that the first child has read the numeral correctly.
- The first child:
  Reads the numeral on the back of the counting card.
  And tells the other child how many objects are buried.
  Finds the objects.
  Places them on the space holders on the card
  And counts them to check.
- Change roles and repeat.

The adult:

- Shows the children how to match objects to space holders on the counting cards.
- Helps the children select an appropriate number of objects for a counting card.
- Helps the children read the numerals.

Things To Think About

Basic Skills: One-to-one matching. Counting skills for one to five objects. Reading numerals.

Drawing Around My Outline

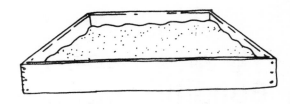

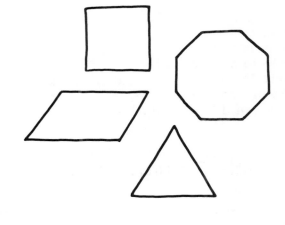

Materials:

- Sandbox full of sand
- Popsicle sticks
- Tools for drawing in sand
- Shapes and objects large enough for the children to trace

Materials Preparation:

- Prepare or locate shapes and objects suitable for the children to trace.

Activity:

The child:

- Selects an object or shape.
- Lays it in the sandbox.
- Traces its outline with a popsicle stick or other tool.
- Removes the object or shape.
- Decorates the object or shape outline.
- Labels the object or shape picture.

The adult:

- Smooths the sand in the sandbox.
- Divides it into areas for children to use.
- Helps children select objects or shapes to trace that are suitable for them.
- Helps children label objects or shapes.

Things To Think About

Make certain there are objects and shapes of varying complexity, so each child will be able to have a successful and challenging experience.

Basic Skills: Tracing around objects and shapes.

Building and Sculpting An Airport

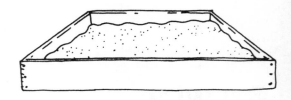

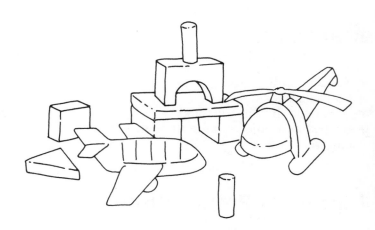

Materials:

- Sandbox
- Airplanes
- Blocks to make buildings
- Molds, buckets, cartons, and other things to make buildings
- Pictures of different airports

Materials Preparation:

- Mix some water into the sand to make it good molding consistency.

Activity:

The children:

- Fill building molds with sand.
- Pat the sand down firmly.
- Turn the carton, cup, or mold over in the sand to make hangars, control towers, terminals, and other airport buildings.
- Use their hands to mold windows and doors in buildings.
- Make runways, roads, parking lots, and driveways.
- Fly airplanes into and out of the airport.
- Pretend to do different jobs at the airport.

The adult:

- Discusses features of an airport.
- Shows pictures of different airports around the world.
- Talks about jobs at the airport.
- Discusses airport size, kinds of planes that land, different-sized airports, number of airlines, and other interesting ideas about them.

Things To Think About

Basic Skills: Learning about the buildings and people which are at an airport. Building a concept of different occupations.

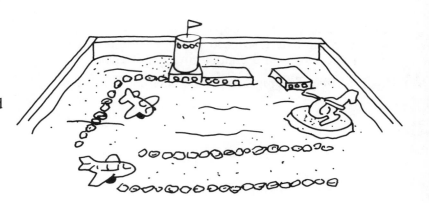

Games
Road Race

3-4 years

Materials:

- Sandbox
- Small wooden or plastic cars
- Large Spoon

Materials Preparation:

None

Activity:

The child:

- Flattens the sand.
- Uses a large spoon to push a car down preformed tracks.
- Races can be timed or children can form teams for relay car races.

The adult:

- Pushes a car several times in the sand to make straight and curved tracks.

Things To Think About

Basic Skills: Pushing and following a straight or curved line.

Building and Sculpting A City

Materials:

- Beach
- Bucket
- Cups or molds (different sizes)
- Milk cartons (different sizes)
- Shells
- Shovels or large spoons
- Pictures of cities

Materials Preparation:

None

Activity:

The children:

- Fill cartons, cups, or molds with sand.
- Pat the sand down firmly and turn molds over in the sand to make houses and buildings in the city.
- Stack molds to make skyscrapers in the city.
- Use shells as doors or roofs to decorate the structures.
- Drag shovels to create roads, parking lots, and driveways.
- Mold fences and roadway dividers with the sand.

The adult:

- Discusses things found in a city.
- Points out where you live on a map.
- Shows pictures of different cities around the world and discusses geography, main occupations, number of inhabitants, popular foods, etc.

Things To Think About

Basic Skills: Learning about the people and places that make up a city.

Movement
Sift and Shout Relay

Materials:

- Beach
- Beach balls
- Sifters
- Assorted molds
- Shovels
- Hoops
- Tall sticks to make goal posts
- One cup measures
- Box big enough to hold a beach ball

Materials Preparation:

- Set up the relay stations as listed below.

Activity:

The children:

- Play Sift and Shout Relay in teams.
  Each child:
- Fills a mold and turns it over onto the sand.
- Rolls the beach ball into the box while seated.
- Kicks the beach ball between the goal posts.
- Throws the beach ball through the hoop either underhand or overhand.
- Fills the one cup measure with sand.
- Pours it into the sifter.
- Shakes it all out.
- Shouts "I'm done! Hooray!"
  The next child begins.
  Continue that way until all the children have had a turn.

The adult:

- Sets up two sets of stations as follows:
  The first station should have molds and shovels.
  The second station should have a beach ball and box on its side.
  The third station should have a beach ball with sticks to kick it through.
  The fourth station should have a beach ball and a hoop to throw it through.
  The fifth station should have a sifter and a one cup measure.
- Puts children in teams of fairly evenly matched skills.
  (If there are an odd number of children, let one child go twice.)

Things To Think About

Do not emphasize winning — just doing your best. The activity can be set up in a sandbox. Have each child take turns going through the relay. Time each child and encourage each to do better on succeeding trials.

Basic Skill: Developing ball handling skills.

ACTIVITIES FOR
FIVE AND SIX YEAR OLDS

Pouring
Stencil Sift

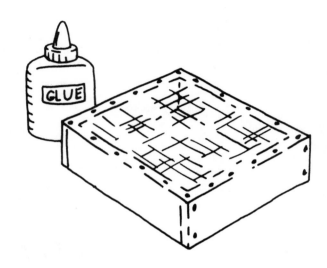

Materials:

- Pan - half full of sand
- Screen in a frame
- Cups
- Dry tempera paint
- School glue
- Paper
- Spoons
- Photos and their negatives

Materials Preparation:

- Place a piece of screen (large enough for sand to go through) in a frame with an inch or two of frame below the screen.

Activity:

The child:

- Pours sand through the screen.
- Uses school glue to fill in areas of the screen to make a design.
- Lets screen dry thoroughly.
- Scoops up sand from the sand pan into a cup.
- Mixes dry tempera into the sand with a spoon.
- Notes that the particles of sand and tempera are different sizes.
- Spreads glue on paper.
- Places screen above paper.
- Pours sand onto screen evenly.
- Taps screen slightly if needed.
- Notes that the areas filled on the screen are not filled on the paper.

The adult:

- Points out that sand comes in different sizes.
- Points out that most of the sand goes through the screen, but some is too large.
- Helps child fill in screen with glue.
- Talks about the screen design as a negative for the paper design.
- Shows some photos and their negatives to help understanding.

Things To Think About

Basic Skills: Learning about comparing sizes. Learning about negatives.

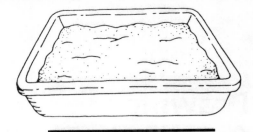

Patting and Molding
Molding a Fish

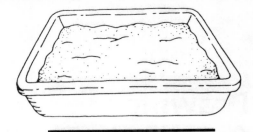

5-6 years

Materials:

- Fish mold
- Deep pan
- Sand
- Fork
- Spoons
- Water

Materials Preparation:

- Mix some water into the sand to make it good molding consistency.

Activity:

The child:

- Fills scoop with sand.
- Pours sand into mold.
- Pats sand into mold with hand.
- Turns mold over.
- Uses a spoon to make more fish scales.
- Uses small dabs of water to reshape fish scales.
- Uses fork to make gills and fins.

The adult:

- Demonstrates how to make scales with a spoon.
- Demonstrates how to make fish gills and fins with fingers or a fork.
- Demonstrates how to reshape or smooth scales using a few drops of water.

Things To Think About

Basic Skills: Pouring, patting, grasping, and patting. Learning concepts of size and sequential order.

Drawing Animals In The Sand

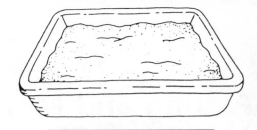

5-6 years

Materials:

- Popsicle sticks
- Deep pan
- Sand
- Animal books

Materials Preparation:

None

Activity:

The child:

- Draws an animal in the sand.
- Other children guess what animal was drawn.
- Decides if animal is warm-blooded or cold-blooded.
- Decides if animal lives in the sea or on the land.

The adult:

- Shows children books of animals from different parts of the world.
- Discusses warm-blooded and cold-blooded animals.
- Discusses the differences in sea animals and land animals.

Things To Think About

Basic Skills: Discussing animal names and categories.

Sand Science
What Is Sand Made Of?

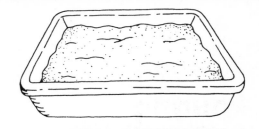

Materials:

- Beach sand, if possible
- Clear cups
- Shells
- White vinegar
- Magnet
- Thin white paper
- Iron ore powder
- Unusual types of sand such as black and green sand from Hawaii

Materials Preparation

None

Activity:

The child:

First:
- Puts sand in a clear cup.
- Covers the sand with white vinegar.
- Looks for bubbles in the liquid.
  If there are bubbles, the sand has limestone or shells in it.

Second:
- Spreads a thin layer of sand on paper.
- Wraps a magnet in paper.
- Moves the magnet over the sand.
  If there are small dark particles in the paper around the magnet, the sand has magnetic iron ore in it.

The adult:

- Helps the child observe the bubbles.
- Points out that sand contains limestone.
- Demonstrates how vinegar bubbles on a shell because the shell contains limestone.
- Shows how a magnet wrapped in paper picks up iron ore.
- Shows other types of sand, if available, and discusses what they are made of.

Things To Think About

Basic Skills: Understanding that sand is made up of many materials.

49

Pouring Measurement

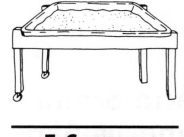

Materials:

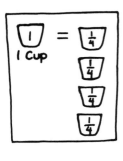

- Sand table
- 2 cup, 1 cup, ½ cup, and ¼ cup measuring cups
- Balance scales
- Chart for recording results

Materials Preparation:

- Make a chart as pictured.
- Make 2 cup, 1 cup, ½ cup, and ¼ cup measuring cups out of construction paper, making each size out of a different color.

Activities:

The child:

- Fills ½ cup measuring cup with sand.
- Pours it into 1 cup measuring cup.
- Fills ½ cup measuring cup with sand again and pours it into 1 cup measuring cup.
- Notes on chart that two ½ cup measuring cups of sand fill a 1 cup measuring cup.
- Uses the one cup measuring cup to fill the ½ cup measuring cup.
- Notes that it takes two times to empty the 1 cup measuring cup into the ½ cup measuring cup.
- Repeats the procedure with ¼ cup into the 1 cup measuring cup.
  and
- Pours measuring cups full of sand on a balance scale.
- Notes that two ½ cup measures of sand balance one 1 cup measure.
- Repeats with other combinations.

The adult:

- Identifies different sized measuring cups.
- Shows children how to put measuring cups on chart to indicate equalities.
- Shows children how to use balance scales.

Things To Think About

For younger children this activity can be done with 1 cup, 2 cup, and 4 cup measuring cups.

Basic Skills: Learning about fractions. Learning about reversibility of fractions.

Patting and Molding Sand Lion

Materials:

• Sand table
• Water
• Popsicle sticks

Materials Preparation:

• Mix some water into the sand to make it good packing consistency.

Activity:

The child:

• Pulls sand together with his hands to create a lion's head.
• Uses fingers, hands, and tools to sculpture the features of the lion.
• Uses his spread fingertips to create a mane around the lion's face.
• Uses straws for whiskers on the lion's face.
• Makes an equal number of whiskers on each side of the lion's face.

The adult:

• Helps the child create a lion's head.
• Helps the child use fingers, hands, and tools to sculpture the features of the lion.
• Helps the child use his spread fingertips to create a mane around the lion's face.
• Helps the child use straws for whiskers on the lion's face.
• Helps the child make an equal number of whiskers on each side of the lion's face.

Things To Think About

A more advanced activity is to have children pretend the lion is a clock, and place numerals on the lion's mane clockface.

Basic Skills: Patting and molding. Sculpting with fingers, hands, and tools. Identifying equal numbers of things.

51

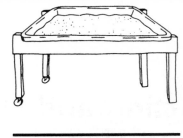

Drawing
Mirror Design

Materials:

- Mirror
- Popsicle sticks
- Sand table
- Sand

Materials Preparation:

None

Activity:

The child:

- Draws a curved line.
- The next child draws the same line in the opposite direction.
- Continue the pairing activity until the children have completed the mirror design.

The adult:

- Demonstrates the meaning of a mirror image: Shows how words look backwards in a mirror; Shows how you draw a design in the mirror and it looks like it has been drawn in the opposite direction.

Things To Think About

Basic Skills: Grasping, drawing, and following a pattern in reverse. Concept of mirror image.

Building Towers and Bridges

Materials:

- Sand table
- Small cups or molds
- Tongue depressors or popsicle sticks
- Water

Materials Preparation:

- Mix some water into the sand to make it good molding consistency.

Activity:

The child:

- Fills molds with sand.
- Packs the sand tightly into the molds.
- Turns the molds over in the sand table one on top of the other to create a tower.
- Makes several towers.
- Counts the number of molds in each tower.
- Puts tongue depressors between molds to other towers to create bridges.
- Counts the number of towers in the structure.
- Counts the number of bridges in the structure.
- Decides which tower is taller or shorter.
- Decides which tower has more molds and more bridges.
- Decides which tower has less molds and less bridges.

The adult:

- Helps the child fill molds.
- Helps the child pack the sand tightly.
- Helps the child turn the molds over in the sand table to create towers.
- Helps the child count the molds as he works.
- Helps the child decide which tower is taller or shorter.
- Helps the child decide which tower has more molds and bridges.
- Helps the child decide which tower has less molds and bridges.

Things To Think About

The child is beginning to count accurately at this stage, but still may need a lot of support. The activity is designed to build fine motor and eye-hand coordination skills. The concreteness of the activity can be used to teach comparatives and counting.

Basic Skills: Developing fine motor skills of filling and patting. Developing eye-hand coordination skills of lining things up when stacking. Creating a tower. Identifying taller and shorter. Identifying more and less. Developing some counting skills.

Castles
Castles and Moats

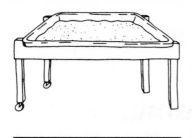

Materials:

- Bucket
- Cups (different sizes)
- Sand table
- Sand
- Scoop or small shovel
- Water
- Pictures of castles with moats

Materials Preparation:

None

Activity:

The child:

- Scoops sand into cups.
- Pats sand tightly into cups.
- Turns sand filled cups over and builds a castle.
- Scoops one scoop of sand into a bucket of water.
- Takes a hand full of sand and water.
- Lets the sand drip off of her hand onto the basic cup castle.
- Repeats this procedure until satisfied with the castle.
- Scoops out a moat around the castle.

The adult:

- Talks about and shows pictures of castles with moats.
- Demonstrates how to make the basic drip procedure with wet sand.
- Describes a moat.

Things To Think About

Basic Skills: Making drips and moats. Building a concept of a castle.

Games
Tic Tac Toe

Materials:

• Sand table
• Popsicle sticks

Materials Preparation:

None

Activity:

The children:

• Form pairs.
• Make a Tic Tac Toe board in the sand table.
• One child draws an **X** on the board with a popsicle stick or finger.
• The other draws an **O** in an open space.
• The play continues this way until one child gets three in a row vertically, horizontally, or diagonally.
• The first child to get three in a row circles them.
• That child is the winner.

The adult:

• Explains the rules of the game.
• Encourages the children to use the full space in the sand table.
• Encourages the children to take turns.
• Encourages the children to follow the rules.

Things To Think About

This game can be played with any two letters or numerals that the children need to practice.

Basic Skills: Following the rules of a game. Practicing letters and numerals.

Drawing Patchwork Quilt

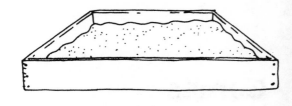

Materials:

- Sandbox full of sand
- Popsicle sticks
- Tools for drawing in sand
- Pictures of simple quilt designs

Materials Preparation:

- Prepare or locate pictures of simple quilt designs such as log cabin and tulip — or create unique ones.

Activity:

The child:

- Selects a quilt design.
- Selects a square in the sandbox.
- Reproduces the design in his square.

The adult:

- Smooths the sand in the sandbox.
- Divides it into one foot squares.
- Helps children select designs that are suitable for them.

Things To Think About

Make certain there are designs of varying complexity, so each child will be able to have a successful, and yet, challenging experience.

Basic Skill: Reproducing designs.

Building and Sculpting
Sculpt a Zoo

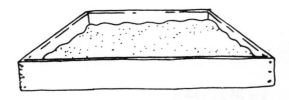

5-6 years

Materials:

- Sandbox
- Toy animals
- Blocks to make buildings
- Molds, buckets, cartons and other things to make buildings
- Pictures of many zoo animals

Materials Preparation:

- Mix some water into the sand to make it good molding consistency.

Activity:

The children:

- Fill building and cage molds with sand.
- Make animal buildings and cages.
- Use their hands to mold windows, doors, and bars in buildings.
- Make natural habitat areas, cages, walkways, roads, parking lots, and driveways.
- Pretend to do different jobs at the zoo.
- Talk about animals in the wild versus animals in a zoo.
- Talk about threatened, endangered, and extinct animals.

The adult:

- Discusses the parts of a zoo.
- Shows pictures of different zoos.
- Talks about jobs at the zoo.
- Discusses the animals.
- Shows pictures of natural habitats of zoo animals.
- Talks about threatened, endangered, and extinct animals.
- Talks about how elephants are being killed for their ivory in Africa.
- Talks about how there are only 900, or so, pandas left in the wild, because man is cutting down their natural habitats.

Things To Think About

Basic Skills: Learning about animals in the wild and in zoos. Learning concepts of threatened, endangered, and extinct.

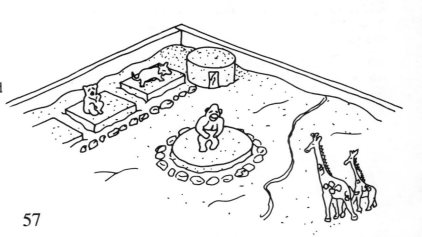

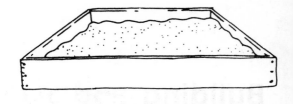

Games
Board Game

Materials:

• Sandbox
• Acorns
• Sticks
• Alphabet cards

Materials Preparation:

• Color acorns different colors.
• Prepare draw cards with letters of the alphabet.

Activity:

The child:

• Designs an alphabet board game with the adult's help.
• Draws a card from the draw pile and moves his game piece to the nearest of that letter shown.
• Another child does the same.
• The winner is the first child to reach the end of the path.

The adult:

• Demonstrates how to make a game in the sand.
• Draws a simple board with letters in the sand.
• Marks start and finish with acorns.
• Uses acorns as game pieces.

Things To Think About

Let children make as much of the gameboard as they can. Use letters you have recently studied. Other suggested game ideas include a shapes game as above, match a shell; mazes; dot-to-dot; or follow the path.

Basic Skills: Drawing, following rules, taking turns, winning and losing, and locating the nearest.

Building and Sculpting A Space Station

5-6 years

Materials:

- Beach
- Bucket
- Cups or molds (different sizes and shapes)
- Milk cartons (different sizes)
- Shells
- Shovels or large spoons
- Pictures of space stations

Materials Preparation:

None

Activity:

The children:

- Fill molds with sand.
- Pat the sand down firmly and turn the carton, cup, or mold over in the sand to make a space station structure.
- Use shells for decorations, doors, roofs, or as the base to place a floating space structure.
- Use shovels to make space craters.
- Drag shovels to create roads, etc.
- Use hands to mold fences, monorails, and sky parking decks.

The adult:

- Discusses space stations.
- Discusses astronauts, space flight, weightlessness, planets, and other information about space travel.
- Shows pictures of space stations.
- Writes a letter to NASA.
- Obtains information about the purpose of space stations.

Things To Think About

Basic Skills: Learning about astronauts, space travel, space stations, flight, weightlessness, planets, life on other planets, etc.

Movement
Who Am I Tracking?

Materials:

• Beach
• Animal track makers
• Animal track cards

Materials Preparation:

• Make animal track makers out of plaster of paris.
• Make animal track activity cards with a picture of the track on one side, the name, a picture of the animal and an activity to imitate the animal on the other side.

    Examples:

Flamingo	Stands on one foot, then the other.
Rabbit	Jumps around.
Dog	Runs on all fours.
Giraffe	Walks tall with hands elevated.
Crocodile	Crawls on all fours and belly.
Horse	Gallops.

• Laminate the animal track cards to protect them.

Activity:

The child:

• Finds a track.
• Identifies the animal.
• Finds the animal track activity card for that animal.
• Imitates the movements of that animal.

The adult:

• Makes animal tracks at different points around the beach.
• Helps children imitate the animal.

Things To Think About

This can be played by laying down pictures of the animals instead of making tracks. This can be conducted as a group activity.

Basic Skill: Developing major muscle groups.

CRAFT ACTIVITIES FOR
THREE THROUGH SIX YEAR OLDS

Sand Painting

3-6 years

Materials:

- Sand
- Dry tempera powder or food coloring
- Shallow tin pan
- Fingerpainting paper
- Plastic mixing jars with lids
- White glue
- Scoop
- Pictures of impressionist paintings

Materials Preparation:

None

Activity:

The child:

- Fills jar with sand.
- Adds either food coloring or dry tempera paint to the sand.*
- Twists the lid onto the jar and shakes it until the sand and color are mixed.
- Continues this procedure until you have several colors of sand each in a different jar.
- Places the fingerpainting paper in the tin pan.
- Spreads white glue onto the fingerpainting paper.
- Sprinkles different colored sand onto areas on the paper.
- When the glue is dry, shakes the picture clear of the excess sand over a box.

* If you use food coloring, dry the sand before proceeding.

The adult:

- Shows children impressionistic paintings.
- Discusses how artists tried to give the illusion of things in that type of art.
- Helps children through the process.

Things To Think About

If they wish to, the children can create a design or picture on the paper with pencil before putting glue on it. Ground colored chalk can be used to color the sand.

Basic skills: Mixing, starting and finishing a project. Creating a design on paper.

Colored Sand In A Jar

3-6 years

Materials:

- Sand
- Dry tempera powder or food coloring
- Plastic mixing jars with lids
- Baby food or small mason jars
- Spoons
- Popsicle sticks
- Pictures of sand dunes

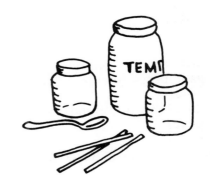

Materials Preparation:

None

Activity:

The child:

- Fills a mixing jar half full of sand.
- Adds either food coloring or dry tempera powder to the sand.
- Twists the lid onto the jar and shakes it until the sand and color are mixed.
- Adds more color if desired.
- Continue this procedure until you have several colors of sand each in a different jar.
- Spoons layers of different colored sand into the baby food jar or mason jar.
- After the layers of colored sand are in the jar, takes the popsicle stick and pushes it in the sand. This will shift the sand and create a sand design.
- Fills sand to the top of the jar so it cannot move once the jar is sealed.

The adult:

- Shows pictures of sand dunes.
- Points out how the dunes are shaped.
- Guides children through the steps of the task.
- Encourages them to make the sand look like dunes.

Things To Think About

Another way to do this activity is to use salt and have the children pulverize colored chalk with a rolling pin as the colorant. Be certain that the jar is filled to the top and has an airtight seal. (The salt will get ruined if moisture seeps in.)

Basic skills: Mixing, starting and finishing a project. Creating a three dimensional design.

Desert Terrarium

Materials:

- Clean sand
- Plastic gallon jugs (one per child)
- Twigs
- Small aloe plants (different types if possible)
- Coarse gravel
- Potting soil
- Attractive rocks, shells or coral formations

Materials Preparation:

- Cut top off of plastic gallon jug or large hole in the side of the plastic jug.

Activity:

The child:

- Places gravel in the bottom of the plastic jug.
- Covers the gravel with 2-3″ of potting soil.
- Covers the potting soil with 2″ of sand.
- Makes holes for two or three aloe plants.
- Plants aloe plants.
- Places rocks, shells, or coral formations in terrarium in a decorative way.
- Talks about amount of rainfall on a desert.
- Moistens soil around the plants.

The adult:

- Points out desert areas on a map.
- Shows pictures of desert areas to the children.
- Helps children plant plants properly.
- Talks about the amount of rainfall on the desert.

Things To Think About

Basic skills: Learning about geography, deserts, and desert plants.

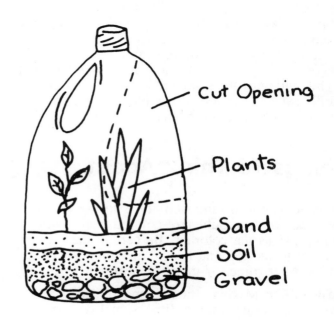

Cut Opening
Plants
Sand
Soil
Gravel